Victims of Apartheid

First seen on BBC-TV in the 1978/79 Play for Today season, *Victims of Apartheid* is the traci-comic story of George O'Brien, a Cape-coloured South African, now living in Ealing. Jobless and deserted by his wife, George turns for help to the preposterous Canon Caper of Christian Underground, an anti-apartheid organisation. Instead the Canon asks George to help Henry, another Cape-coloured refugee. Suspicious of Henry's strange behaviour and haunted by memories of being tortured in South Africa, George fails even to find consolation with Carrie, his Cockney girl-friend. He eventually decides to take his own drastic measures in the fight against apartheid ...

Play for Today
Published in association with BBC-TV, this series includes the scripts of *all* the autumn '78 Plays for Today. Each volume is published simultaneously with first transmission. A list of titles appears overleaf.

The cover photograph shows John Kani as George, Coral Atkins as Carrie and John Matshikiza as Henry in the BBC-TV production of *Victims of Apartheid*, produced by Richard Eyre and directed by Stuart Burge.
BBC Copyright photograph by John Green.

The **Play for Today** series

Tom Clarke

Victims of Apartheid

EYRE METHUEN · LONDON
in association with BBC-TV

First published in 1978 by Eyre Methuen Ltd
11 New Fetter Lane, London EC4P 4EE
Copyright © 1978 by Tom Clarke
Filmset by Northumberland Press Ltd, Gateshead, Tyne & Wear
Printed in Great Britain by Richard Clay (The Chaucer Press) Ltd,
Bungay, Suffolk

ISBN 0 413 45590 4

Victims of Apartheid was first shown on BBC-TV in the 1978/1979 season of Play for Today. The cast was as follows:

GEORGE	John Kani
MOKWE	Lionel Ngakane
CANON CAPER	Peter Jeffrey
HENRY	John Matshikiza
ZAZIE	Mona Hammond
LILY	Peggy Phango
BUS CONDUCTOR	Trevor Laird
BARBARA	Jacquie Cook
CARRIE	Coral Atkins
SANDRA	Norma West
OBED	Oscar James
BILLIE	Holly Wilson
DOCTOR FITZPATRICK	William Hoyland
DOCTOR BANNERJEE	Jamila Massey
JASON	Philip Barker
SUMA	Cynthia Powell
CLARA	Minah Bird
FIRST VOICE	Jacob Witkin
SECOND VOICE	Ken Barker

Designer	Barry Newberry
Producer	Richard Eyre
Director	Stuart Burge

1. Interior. George's flat. Living room. Day.

We open with a fairly tight shot of George. He is South African but not very black, being a Cape coloured. He's wrapped in a blanket. He wears shirt and trousers. The gas fire is alight. He might be rolled in a tribal robe on the veldt with the embers of his cooking fire aglow beside him and dawn breaking over the Drakensberg, but he isn't; he's in W.5, and the transistor which stands on the carpet beside him is burbling. It may be assumed that it's been playing all night. The sound of the doorbell reaches us from the corridor. It fails to waken him. Neither, of course, does a fainter second bell as Mokwe presses the bell of the flat downstairs. Neither does the sound of the front door being opened, nor the sound of voices, nor footsteps ascending the stairs, nor, even, a thunderous knocking on the door of the room. A second insistent knocking succeeds in arousing him. He wakes reluctantly, grimacing, muttering and blinking away at crud-stuck eyes. He crawls out of his blanket, gets to his feet and totters to the door of the room. In doing so he passes a second man asleep on the moquette sofa. A white man, his blond head appears from the satin eiderdown in which he's wrapped. A canvas bag lies against one arm of the sofa, garments are strewn across the floor around the sofa and an empty bottle of Cape brandy lies on its side.

2. Interior. Corridor. Day.

Stairs rise from the ground floor half way along the corridor between the living room in the front and the bedrooms and bathroom which are situated at the rear. There's a gate across the staircase to keep out the downstairs' children, one of whom, Jason, is swinging on it. The kitchenette almost faces the stairs. George opens the door of the living room. Mokwe makes a move to enter, but George counters.

GEORGE. They gone, man. They all gone.

MOKWE. I know they gone. I turn them out myself last night. You don't remember that?

George shakes his head but stands aside for Mokwe to enter.

3. Interior. Living room. Day.

Mokwe enters with George behind him. They stand looking down at the slumbering Ruinek. Mokwe shakes the man.

MOKWE. Come on, Freedom Fighter, you got to carry on the battle somewhere else.

The man opens his eyes, shudders and rolls off the sofa. He crawls to his feet. He's wearing a pair of Y-fronts with aggressively male chauvinist inscriptions on them. He staggers out of the room.

GEORGE. My God, you see what he had on his knickers?

Mokwe looks at him sternly.

MOKWE. All right, George. You going to get ready?

GEORGE. Don't be in such a hurry, man. Sit down. I make some tea. We can have a talk.

Mokwe glances round the room. There are empty bottles and glasses and filled saucers doing duty as ashtrays on every flat surface. The party feeling is further enhanced by the Christmas decorations with which the room is hung, though time has debilitated them. Faded paper-chains, deflated balloons and browning holly hang in sagging festoons, while a Christmas tree displays skeletal branches on which glass baubles and fairy lights are hung. Around it on the floor is a carpet of brown and shrivelled pine-needles.

MOKWE. You got to get this place cleaned up.

George looks round as well. He seems to see no urgency in the situation. He pats his pockets for a cigarette.

MOKWE. You got to take down the decorations and get the place decent.

George finds an empty packet, looks into it and then flings it into the fireplace.

GEORGE. You got a cigarette?

MOKWE. We in April, man, and still you got them up. That's terrible. You got no consciousness of you' surroundin's?

GEORGE. Smoked my last cigarette, Mokwe. You got one?

Mokwe takes out a packet. George takes a cigarette. Mokwe lights it for him and replaces the packet without taking one.

MOKWE. You get this place clean like a new pin. You get that Ruinek out of here. You get fix up with Mr Barton and then we on the road, man.

George has gone over and sat himself down in the armchair by the fire. He's putting his shoes on. He makes no reply.

MOKWE. You remember that, hey? You remember how you promise my Lily last night?

George shakes his head.

GEORGE. Tomorrow. I'll go tomorrow.

MOKWE. Tomorrow is too late. Mr Barton going to keep that job for you till five-thirty today. After that he got to look for someone else.

GEORGE. I can't take that job, Mokwe. (*Mokwe shows no surprise. He's been expecting this.*) I can't take that job, my friend. It's a matter of my principles involved.

MOKWE. You know any bleddy Marxist comrade going to make you foreman at seventy pound a week? Forget you' principles, man. Take the job.

George shakes his head.

GEORGE. Barton wants to put me foreman over those Paki bricklayers because he knows that if he put a white man in there that white man going to the Union and the Union going to black the site. If he brings in a Paki foreman the other Pakis stop work and start arguments. Now you see why I can't take that job. I'd be a blackleg, man, and a bleddy racialist into the bargain.

MOKWE. You want you' wife to come back to you or you want to go on like this?

George looks round the room. He sighs.

GEORGE. You know me, man. You know me. Hell, man, I got a lot of fight in me yet. (*There's a short silence. George frowns, thinking.*) The Canon. I'll go and see the Canon.

MOKWE. How's he going to help you? The Canon got no jobs for you. He's given out all the jobs he's got.

GEORGE. I got something to put to him going to open his eyes, man. I got a new plan. (*He jumps up and throws an arm round Mokwe's shoulders.*) You'll see, you'll see. (*Mokwe looks doubtful.*) You go tell Zazie I got all these fellows cleared out of the flat. You tell her I'm getting the place cleaned up. Like new. And you tell her I got a new job with the Canon.

MOKWE. When you got it, I'll tell her. When you got it.

4. Interior. Offices. Christian Underground. Day.

A corridor with office doors leading off it. On the walls a series of posters urging the condemnation of apartheid, racialism, starvation, oppression, exploitation and the suppression of civil liberties among the deprived peoples of the world. At the foot of each poster the title of the organisation: 'Christian Underground'. The tone of each poster is aggressive in the extreme. A row of straight-backed chairs faces an office door. Seated on one of these chairs is Henry, a light-skinned Cape coloured young man in his early twenties. He's plump, shy, moon-faced, doe-eyed. He wears a long overcoat of the kind favoured by commercial travellers of the nineteen-thirties, and a wild mop of curly hair. The door facing him bears a legend: 'Director of operations – Canon Caper, D.D.' A signwriter, kneeling before the door, is adding the letters 'C.B.E.' to the Canon's distinctions. From within the office we can hear the boom of the Canon's voice. From the other offices comes the clatter of typewriters and the ringing of telephones. This is clearly a busy and prosperous organisation.

5. Interior. Canon Caper's office. Day.

Our attention is drawn to a large coloured poster. It shows a band of liberation fighters making its way through dense jungle. They're clad in steel helmets and camouflage clothing. Large in the foreground, caught in a half-crouch as he parts the undergrowth, is their leader, wary, ferocious and very black. This formidable negro is armed, not with the obligatory automatic weapon, but with a crucifix which he holds extended in one hand as if to exorcise the evil forces against which he and his followers are about to do battle. The crucifix radiates a brilliant glow. In large letters above this lurid scene is the legend: 'The Christian Underground', while stencilled across it in that type usually found on packing cases the words: 'Forward to Freedom'. Seated below this poster is Canon Caper himself. A young fifty, curly-haired, vital, muscular and keen-eyed. His clothing consists of a stained – battle-stained, perhaps – tropical bush-jacket with bulging pockets which we might well imagine could do duty as ammunition pouches. His trousers, thigh-clinging whipcord, are thrust into calf-length mosquito boots. His desk is large and furnished with an office intercom, an electronic calculator, an array of telephones and the varied impedimenta of the business tycoon. At a second desk a pretty secretary sits at her typewriter. On the wall facing the Canon are a number of maps, studded with magnetic coloured buttons, graphs and charts. They refer to such matters as the millions of pounds appealed for and received by the Underground, ecclesiastical bodies affiliated to it, numbers of political prisoners held by each country where the Underground operates, and other visualisations of the Canon's interests and activities. Facing the Canon, seated on a hard chair designed to discomfit interviewees, sits George. George wears a smart suit and sober tie. The Canon is speaking on the telephone.

CANON (*on telephone*) ... Oh, no, on Thursday afternoon. They ... (*with some self-conscious emphasis on his technical know how*) ... *tape* these shows, you know. Well, I am, naturally. It'll be a peak-hour transmission on the following Sunday ... that's it, to catch the *ratings*. That's frightfully important in the media. Well, thanks, old chap, I'm sure your turn will come. Regards to your good Lady. I'll doubtless see you at the Ecumenical. 'Bye, now. (*He replaces the telephone and grins affably at George.*) How are you, George. Awfully good to see you. And your wife? Lulu, isn't it?

GEORGE. Zazie, Canon. She's fine, fine ...

CANON. And what can we do for you? By the way, you probably saw the young fellow waiting outside. Young ... (*He glances down at his desk*.) ... young Grootkamp. I want to talk to you about him. Only arrived yesterday and utterly lost and disoriented, poor fellow. Most providential, your popping in this morning ...

GEORGE. Canon, I want to ask you a question. Would you not agree that the Anti-Apartheid movement is widely dispersed?

CANON. Widely dispersed? How do you mean?

GEORGE. I mean, all over the place. You got United Nations in New York, you got OAU, you got NAACP, you got your lobbies here, in Washington, in Moscow even ...

The Canon is looking at George with increasing suspicion. He interrupts him.

CANON. You're not proposing another fund-raising tour, are you, George?

GEORGE. Fund raising? Good Lor' no, Canon.

CANON. Because funds are the least of our worries. They are, in fact, an embarrassment. What with the Vorster Government banning us in South Africa and the World Council of Churches vetoing our arms-buying programme, it's a real problem to know best how to employ the very generous contributions which are constantly flowing in. There is Chile, Catholics, of course, but with the Ecumenical ...

GEORGE. Canon, what I'm about to suggest could well resolve that problem for you.

George stands smiling at the Canon who appears apprehensive. George pulls out a pair of heavy-rimmed glasses and puts them on. His manner becomes oratorical.

Who you get representing Christian Underground at these centres of resistance? You got a delegate at United Nations? You got a man at the Organisation of African Unity?

CANON. Not precisely, but I, myself, of course ...

GEORGE. No, Canon, you aren't taking my meaning. You're the Director, you're the brains of the organisation. But the brain can't work without the Intelligence. What you need, Canon, is a man who can keep you informed. A man who knows how to keep his ears open. A man who's got experience of the internal politics of the various pressure groups. A man with intimate knowledge of the main personalities involved. Listen to me, Canon. You employ me as roving delegate and I keep you supplied with the real inside information. That way you can persuade people to do what you want. Just take Matuzato. They considering him for Ambassador to UNO. Listen, I can tell you things about Matuzato so when he gets up in the General Assembly and addresses the Delegates of All Nations he speaks with your mouth. He speaks for you and for Christian Action, and by God, if he don't we can fix him so he don't speak for nobody. Canon, what I got on that Matuzato ...

George laughs with pleasure and stares eagerly at the Canon. The latter shakes his head.

CANON. I'm afraid, George, we could hardly consider anything which was not strictly ...

GEORGE. Wait. Wait. What I'm talking about is strictly under cover. You appoint me Official Representative and I do just what all such representatives do. I make speeches. I attend conferences. I address seminars. I appear on TV. And I got the qualifications, too. I was on TV all over Europe when I was on the fund-raising tour. You remember that? I been interviewed on TV by Ludovic Kennedy. I'm speaking at Public Meetings every week. Every ex-detainee comes to this country visits my house. I know everybody in the movement. And I got a prison record second to none. All right, Obed got a longer sentence, but I stood up to the SBs for thirty-six days. Thirty-six days continuous interrogation, Canon ...

The Canon has risen and come round his desk. He flings an arm round George's shoulder.

CANON. I know, George, I know. What you fellows have suffered at the hands of ...

But George is not to be stopped. He twists out of the Canon's grasp and dodges round the corner of the desk, snatching his glasses off.

GEORGE. ... thirty-six days, Canon. Thirty-six days. The things they did to me! (*Clinging to the Canon's desk he leans forward, eyes blazing with excitement.*) Listen, man, you ever stop to think what it's like to have your penis nailed to the table? (*The Canon flashes an apprehensive glance towards his secretary.*) On tip toe I had to stand, with a bleddy great nail through my member! (*He positions himself against the edge of the desk, rising on tiptoe in graphic illustration of the past indignity.*) Five hours on tiptoe, man. Five hours on tiptoe and I got weak ankles! (*George slowly relaxes, dropping his voice.*) Five hours I'm standing there, trying not to think what's going to happen if my ankles give way. All right, Obed done seven years on Robben Island and I got only three, but that was because I was done under the Explosives Act. They couldn't get the Terrorism Act through Parliament in time to catch me with it. (*He shakes his head.*) Thirty-six days before I made a statement. That's a record.

> *The Canon manages to resume control. He again puts his arm round George's shoulder.*

CANON. Don't think, George, that I don't understand how difficult it is for someone like you to accept that his part in the fight for freedom is over ... (*George shows signs of resentment. The Canon adds quickly:*) ... for the time being. For the time being, of course. But George, you're entitled to a respite. You're entitled to take a back seat for a while, pursue your career, enjoy your home and family ...

GEORGE. I don't want to enjoy my bleddy home and family. I been taking a back seat for five years in this country! I want to get back into the fight, man. Listen, why don't you get me back to South Africa? Fix me up with a dog-collar and a black suit. Get me in through Swaziland or Bophutswana. You can do it, man. Drop me by bleddy parachute, I don't care. (*He strides up to the poster.*) I tell you, Canon, you get me back there and I'll give those bastards more than a bleddy crucifix.

> *George gives a bark of laughter. The Canon, mortally offended, turns his back on George and walks to the window, trying to control his temper. George tries to make amends.*

I'm sorry, Canon. To you that's like some kind of Holy Death Ray. I respect that, Canon, truly. You done a whole lot of good work with that thing.

The Canon turns.

CANON. George, you and your kind are Front Line troops and I'm, well, I'm only the old Padre back at base. But George, we all have to serve in our own way.

GEORGE. That's right, Padre, to each according to his ability, to each according to his ...

CANON. Well, yes, something like that. And that's why, George, I'm asking you to take young Grootkamp under your wing.

GEORGE. Grootkamp?

CANON. The young man outside. You'll remember, I mentioned him. He came in on a flight only yesterday ...

GEORGE. Just one moment, Canon. You got to watch your step with these people. They got blacks in the Special Branch specially trained as infiltrators. You remember that ...

CANON. There's no doubt about this young chap, George, he comes with the highest recommendations from his Pastor. He has gone through a great deal, it seems, and is in urgent need of help. We've got to take him in hand, George. Set him on his feet again, as we've done with so many others with the help of people like yourself. What do you say?

GEORGE. Okay, Canon, if you say he's a victim of apartheid, that's good enough for me.

CANON. Splendid, George, splendid. I knew I could rely on you ... (*His hand dives into his jacket pocket and comes out with his wallet.*) Now, something towards expenses.

The Canon flutters notes in front of George. George steps back.

GEORGE. No, Canon, no. I wouldn't hear of it. You been very generous to me already. No, I won't take your money, Canon.

CANON. You're a brick, George, a brick. But we can't ask the good Lulu to give the young chap bed and board for nothing. It does fall on the wives, this kind of thing. We have to think of the wives, George.

GEORGE. You want me to put him up at my place, Canon?

CANON. As you've so generously done with so many in the past. Of course, if, for some reason it's inconvenient ...

George looks at him miserably

GEORGE. It's not exactly inconvenient, but ...

CANON. Splendid.

He pushes the money into George's hand and ushers him to the door.

6. Interior. Corridor. Day.

Henry looks up in alarm and rises slowly to his feet as the Canon precedes George out of his office.

CANON. I know he'll be in good hands.

He stands aside to allow George to pass him.

(*To Henry.*) You'll be in good hands with George here, old chap. You go along with George. He's going to take you under his wing. (*Henry and George inspect each other warily.*) Well, cheers, chaps. All the best to both of you.

The Canon raises a hand in farewell. Henry starts to move along the corridor. George follows him. The Canon withdraws into his room. But before he's actually closed the door George turns.

GEORGE. Canon. I should explain. They don' drive the nail right through the centre of course. They pinch off a piece of the skin to one side ...

The Canon closes his door.

7. Interior. George's house. Kitchenette. Day.

A large black lady, Lily, Mokwe's wife, has her back to us staring into the kitchenette. A murmur of disbelief escapes her:

LILY. My God ... My God in Heaven ...

A shout turns her round. It comes from Zazie who stands in the doorway to the living room. Zazie is a handsome light-coloured woman, an African with Indian or Malaysian blood.

ZAZIE. Lily, Lily, will you come here ...

Lily turns, walks along the passage and follows Zazie into the living room.

8. Interior. Living room. Day.

Zazie waves a hand towards the faded decorations.

ZAZIE. You ever see anything like this? You ever in you' life?

LILY. You look at the kitchen, Zazie. Just go look at the kitchen see what he done with you' blender.

ZAZIE. He has not touched this place since New Year. New Year morning I get up out my bed and comes in here and what I find him doin'? That man standin' there at the window. Window wide open, freezin' cold. And he urinatin' out the window. (*She turns a look of outrage at Lily.*) What downstairs goin' to think of that, man? (*Lily shakes her head.*) Lily, what am I goin' to do? When I think I got to give up my comfort and my freedom, livin' with my Chloe in peace and quiet and come back here to that man, that crazy man ... (*Zazie looks at Lily and smiles.*) There a man round there, in next door flat. He speakin' very civil to me, man. When I come off night duty, I goin' in, him comin' out. We pass in the entrance hall. 'How are you, Mrs O'Brien,' he say. 'Very well, thank you,' I say. Very polite, very pleasant.

Lily gives a screech.

LILY. Zazie! What you sayin'!

ZAZIE. I'm not sayin' anythin'. Except there's benefits for me too, livin' on my own. (*She casts a glance round the room.*) He not got all the benefits, man.

She sighs resignedly, turns and leads the way out of the room.

9. Exterior. Bus stop. Street. Day.

A bus pulls up and a woman descends. In doing so she casts a curious look backwards. George and Henry seated on the bench next to the platform. Henry is squashed into a corner and looks terrified. He wears a rolled-up balaclava helmet. He nurses a huge suitcase on his knee. George is next to him, his body hunched and tense, exuding hostility. The bus starts to pull away.

10. Interior. Bus. Day.

The Conductor, a Jamaican, stands in front of George. George holds out two tenpenny pieces and holds up two fingers. The Conductor gives him tickets. He glances at Henry.

CONDUCTOR. Just off the boat?

George affects not to hear. The Conductor has a cockney accent.

Your mate. Just off the boat, is he?

George gives the Conductor a surly look.

GEORGE. My friend is a refugee. A refugee from South Africa. A victim of apartheid.

The Conductor is suitably awestricken.

CONDUCTOR. Cor! What they do to him? He looks terrible.

George gives a hollow laugh.

GEORGE. He's scared shitless, man. He thinks he's going to be arrested for sitting with white folks. Can't get used to the idea there's no colour bar in this country. (*The Conductor gives a shout of derisive laughter. George looks at him sternly.*) There is no colour bar in this country. In this country there is racialism, but there is no colour bar.

The Conductor gives him a long look.

CONDUCTOR. You got racialism, who needs a colour bar.

And he moves off before George can reply. George turns and looks at Henry. His expression relaxes some of its hostility.

GEORGE. I know how you feel, man. My God, I felt the same myself. The first time I got on a bus in this country, sitting all amongst the white chickies, man, I had a hard on all the way from Victoria Station to Russell Square.

He grins and looks round. His eyes encounter a White Chickie on the seat opposite. She radiates disapproval. George seems not to notice it, but drops his voice a shade. He looks up, catches the White Girl's eye on him and gives her a smile of pure friendliness. Her disapproval is swamped by her confusion. George slaps Henry's suitcase with the palm of his hand. He says:

(in Afrikaans). Come on, man, we get off here.

And rises.

11. Interior. Corridor. Day.

George comes out of the living room and makes his way to the kitchenette. The child Jason stands on the top step of the stairs by the low gate. Unwashed, its face smeared with foodstuff, wearing only a darned vest, he clutches a wooden toy. George expresses irritation:

GEORGE. Jason, go down your own part of the house.

The Child stares at him gravely. George glances downwards to assure himself that the coast is clear, and aims a swipe at the Child's head. The Child ducks expertly.

Go down, you little bastard.

George goes into the kitchenette. As he does so the Child hurls his toy at him. It catches George in the back of the leg. George swears. The Child screams with delight and disappears down the stairs.

12. Interior. Kitchenette. Day.

The kitchenette, originally a broom-cupboard now slightly enlarged, is fitted up with all the latest electrical and culinary apparatus. This wealth of labour-saving device is almost invisible under the accumulated debris of George's bachelorhood. Dirty dishes, pots, pans, cutlery and glasses, together with empty and half-empty milkbottles and partly emptied cans and cartons of food, occupy every available surface and are piled in the sink. George appears to notice nothing amiss. He stretches over the debris, lifts a kettle from the stove, fills it and puts it back on the stove. He turns the gas on and lights it.

13. Interior. Living room. Day.

Henry is sitting in one of the two armchairs which, together with a settee, make up the three-piece suite. He has kept his overcoat on. George enters.

GEORGE. Take your coat off, man.

HENRY (*in Afrikaans*). It's cold.

GEORGE. How can you say it's cold. It's April. In this country April is springtime. You got to acclimatise yourself, man. (*He stoops and turns the tap on the elaborate and modern gas heater which immediately lights itself.*) You got thin blood. Well, we soon get you used to this climate.

Henry moves forward in his chair, hunching himself over the glow from the fire. George looks down on him with commiseration.

Look, Henry, I know how you feelin', man. When they let me out from Robben Island I wouldn't speak to *anybody*. Even to Zazie I didn't speak. Zazie's my wife. (*He gives a swift and slightly furtive glance round the room.*) Three years' solitary confinement! After that you don't feel loquacious! But it's better to talk. It's better for your own sake. You get it off you' chest. You feel better.

Henry stirs restlessly, glances up at George and gives him a weak smile. But he says nothing. George frowns and takes a pace up and down the room. He comes back and stands looking down at his guest.

GEORGE. You make a statement? Is that what's worrying you? Listen, man, there's nothing to be ashamed of in that. Everybody makes a statement in the end. If a man tell you different he's a liar. Nothing to be ashamed of. You want to forget it.

*Henry mutters something, but George has already moved away and
seized one of the three stools from the veneer-and-plastic bar which has
been set in one corner of the room, glass shelves let into the wall behind
it, bare of any but purely decorative glassware. George takes the stool to
the centre of the room and climbs up onto it.*

When I gave in and agreed to make a statement they took me into
this special room. They got a table and some chairs and they got this
stool. Just like this one, only maybe a bit higher. (*He glances around at
Henry to assure himself of his attention.*) You got to sit wit' you' legs
straight out each side, not touchin' the floor. (*He demonstrates.*) And
you' arms the same, straight out sideways. (*George stretches his arms out
at a downward angle, resembling a figure by Blake.*) So you just restin' on
you' arse, balancin' see? In front of you they got a psychiatric expert.
He's got a list of the questions you goin' to be asked. But he don't ask the
question. Behind you is two Special Branch men. You can't see them.
They ask the questions. The psychiatrist watches you' face when you
answer each question. He marks down you' reactions, see. Each
question, he makes a note on the paper. They go through these
questions and then they take you away. Next day you do it all over
again. For ten days they do it. Some of the questions are crazy, 'What
you' name? What you' father's name? Where you go to school?' Crazy.
But you got to answer, same as the other questions. 'Who you' contact
in Jo'burg? Where you' letter box? How you get explosive?' They mix
'em up, these questions. And if you get tired and let you' arms drop
the feller behind you he fetch you a buffet on the head. Oh, man, you
learn to sit still and answer the questions. (*He sits quite still, smiling
again at the devilish ingenuity of his past persecutors. Then, gravely:*)
They put the questions very polite.

*George gets off the stool and replaces it at the bar. He walks over and
sits down on the settee, facing Henry.*

Swanepoel was my Chief Interrogator. You ever heard of him,
Major Swanepoel? (*Henry shakes his head.*) What a bastard! That
man was known to every brother in the Movement. Major Swanepoel.
He been to Sandhurst College for his trainin'. Trained over here by the
British. Then they sent him to Northern Ireland for his practical
trainin' in the field. By Ghod, by the time he got back to South Africa
that man knew all the tricks. (*He walks over and puts a hand on Henry's*

shoulder.) Well, that's all done with. You got nothing to fear now, man. You in England now. They got no SB's here. (*He grins*.) So long you don't get mixed up with those Irish bastards you got nothing to fear in this country.

From the kitchen comes a piercing whistle as the kettle boils. George hurries out of the room. Henry gets up and examines the books on the shelves set into the right-hand side of the chimney-breast. They're mostly political works, and books dealing with the Anti-Apartheid movement, but there's a sprinkling of romantic fiction. On one of the lower shelves there's a pile of dog-eared exercise books. Henry takes the top one of these and opens it. Behind him George returns with two mugs of tea. Henry replaces the exercise book.

Ah, you' looking at my book. You' welcome to read it, but I got to get it typed when I can get some cash collected together.

He walks past Henry and lifts out the pile, eight or nine exercise books. George walks over to the square dining-table which is pushed against the wall between the two windows and plops them down. He stands looking at them.

I promised myself I'd get on with that while Zazie's away – she's gone on holiday – but, I don't know, I don't seem to settle to it properly. Of course, I get a lot of friends comin' round, and ... (*He looks at Henry a little sheepishly*.) With Zazie out of the house I been livin' a bit of a Bohemian life, tell you the truth. (*in Afrikaans*) What did you get picked up for.

HENRY (*in Afrikaans*). I never was picked up.

George stares at him disbelievingly.

GEORGE. You telling me you never once in you' life been arrested? (*Henry shakes his head. George's incredulity increases*.) You mean you never once been caught without you' pass book? You never been picked up in a house-to-house sweep? You never been stopped in a prohibited area? (*Henry shakes his head again*.) They never got you under the Urban Areas Act, or Influx Control, or Unlawful Assembly, of Insulting Words and Behaviour?

HENRY. No.

So positive a denial is almost an act of aggression. George takes a pace towards him.

GEORGE. That's just not credible, man. A black man of your years and you say you never been arrested? I tell you it's not credible.

He stares at Henry who does his best to appear something other than statistically abnormal. George advances on him threateningly.

You workin' for the SBs. (*He searches Henry's face for signs of guilt.*) You a bleddy police spy come over here to infiltrate the Anti-Apartheid movement. You pickin' up information on the Canon. My Ghod, you done a good job, too. You got that man eatin' out of you' hand.

Henry shakes his head violently.

HENRY (*in Afrikaans*). No, that's not true ...

GEORGE. Oh! Maybe you' a bleddy double agent? You workin' for the Canon too. The Canon tell you to find out if I'm a Party Member? I can tell you, you barkin' up the wrong tree there. I'm no bleddy Stalinist, man! Me, a Party Member! You makin' me laugh. I was elected to the Council on the Labour Party ticket. A Marxist, yes, I'm a Marxist ... What you doin'? (*Henry has got to his feet, stooped and picked up his suitcase. George repeats his question:*) What you think you' doin'?

HENRY. I better go.

George is visibly taken aback. But he recovers himself.

GEORGE. Go? Where you think you' goin'? You go so many friends in this country you ... (*A thought strikes him.*) You goin' back to the Canon? (*Henry stares at him defiantly.*) Oh, no you don't. You not runnin' back to that man tellin' him I let him down. I got an obligation to that man to set you up on you' feet.

George and Henry glare at each other. George is the first to soften. He gestures:

Put you' case down, man. We got to work on this together. I got to think about what you tol' me. I got to think out what to do.

George studies Henry intently. Henry bears the inspection with fortitude. At length:

Come on, I'll show you where you can sleep. Then we go out. I'll take you round the local. That will open your eyes, man. A proper pub, not like the bleddy low-life shebeens they got in the townships back there.

He holds the door open and Henry passes through.

14. Interior. Saloon bar. Day.

One of those large bleak rooms characteristic of suburban public houses. Circular tables with chairs set round them. A window with drab and dusty curtains glazed with frosted glass in the lower pane so as to prevent anyone passing by in the street catching sight of those drinking within. A solitary white Working-Man in painter's overalls is contemplating a pint glass at one of the tables, while at a second table sit three silent and motionless Women, three serge-coated harpies mulling over the inadequacies of their share of their husbands' pay packets. A pace or two from the Painter stands Henry. He holds a full pint glass in his hand. He too is motionless. Geroge's voice breaks the silence. His voice reflects warmth, friendliness and consideration.

GEORGE (*off*). Sit down. Sit down, man.

George walks into picture. He's smiling, brimming with good nature. He carries a pint glass. He gestures towards the vacant chairs at the Painter's table.

Take the weight off you' feet, man.

Henry doesn't move. George takes his seat, placing his pint on the table. He looks up at Henry and gestures to the vacant chair opposite him.

What's the matter, man? Sit down.

The Painter has been regarding George with some distaste. George turns to him.

My friend's only shortly arrived in this country. He's from South Africa. In South Africa, to sit down with a white man ...

The Painter, giving George a look of disgust, picks up his glass, gets to his feet and removes himself from the scene. Henry, having assured himself that the coast is clear, takes his place. Meanwhile:

... is actually a criminal offence. In a public place, that is.

*George frowns after the retreating Painter and falls momentarily silent.
But not for long. He speaks severely to Henry.*

You won't get along like that, you know. That man could see your
embarrassed as well. Racialism is founded on the colour-consciousness
of the black. You got to get it in you' thick head, man.

*He lifts his glass. Henry does likewise. Henry sips, makes a face
indicating disgust and puts his glass down very firmly. George
contemplates Henry over the top of his glass. The barmaid, Barbara,
appears, picks up Henry's glass and wipes the table with a cloth.*

Hello, Borbora. How are you today, sweetie?

Barbara, a hard-faced blonde of ample proportions glances at George.

I want you to meet my friend here. He's just arrived from South
Africa. Henry, this is Borbora. The Irish Rose, that's what I call her,
isn't that right, Borbora?

*Barbara acknowledges the introduction with a snort and moves away.
George calls after her.*

How's the boyfriend, eh? Still bringing you those little presents, is he?
(*He turns to Henry.*) Her boyfriend's a steward on the British Rail
Dining Cars.

*George gazes out of picture at the charms of the invisible Barbara. Then
he suddenly jumps up.*

Some friends of mine ...

*Henry watches as George makes his way towards the bar. The room has
begun to fill up. George joins a Group of half a dozen or so people.
George speaks to them. Heads are turned in Henry's direction. Henry
squirms with embarrassment. George, his arm round the waist of a white
Woman in her late thirties, conducts the Group over to Henry.*

Here we are. This is Henry. Henry I want you to meet Sandra.
Sandra's from the Cape, too.

*Sandra smiles at Henry, who half rises in his chair to be pushed down
again by George.*

Sandra was married to one of the top brain surgeons in the Cape.

SANDRA. Oh, George, shut up.

George grins.

GEORGE. She doesn't want me to tell you about it. Listen, the cops caught her in the back of her old man's car with the chauffeur, a big Zulu. Only because her old man got it hushed up they didn't do her in under the Immorality Act. How much that cost your old man, Sandra, hey?

SANDRA. George! Honestly, you're unreal!

Sandra gives George a playful shove. She sits down next to Henry. George introduces the others.

GEORGE. Obed ... Obed, come here. Meet Henry, Obed. Just arrived in this country. And this is wife Suma, and this is his wife Billie, and this is his new wife, Clara. And this is Stanley – he's Sandra's friend – and Carrie and her friend Betty, this is Henry, Carrie, and this is John, Big John we call him ...

They crowd round, some sitting down, some fetching chairs from other tables. Sandra's plump and Jewish, well but flashily dressed. Obed's a huge African wearing a tribal robe over a neat blue suit, club tie and brilliantly polished shoes, Billie's his English wife, a Somerville girl, Suma is one of his two African ones, and wears African dress. Clara, the third wife, is also African, and a knockout, tall, and wears very trendy and revealing clothes. Stanley's an English civil servant and much younger than Sandra, Carrie's a dark cockney girl in her early thirties in whom emaciation has not yet destroyed her attractiveness and Betty's a scrawny blonde. Big John's a construction foreman home on leave from Kuwait.

15. Interior. Saloon bar. Night.

Everyone is seated and the Group has grown by three or four. Everyone has had a good deal to drink and there's a tendency towards hilarity. It being well past closing time, Barbara is chivvying other customers out of the bar, giving a glance across at George's Group now and then, an

*indication that she sees a possible battle to come. She approaches them,
radiating aggression but masking it behind a show of publican's bonhomie:*

BARBARA. Come along now, come along. Well past your bedtimes.
Come along, haven't you people got homes?

George sways to his feet.

GEORGE. I got a home, Barbara, I got a home, and you' welcome any
time. How about it, Barbara? You coming home with me.

*Carrie gives a shriek and grabs George's coat, dragging him back into
his seat beside her.*

CARRIE. Oo! D'you hear that. George, you cheeky bugger!

George struggles to his feet again, shedding Carrie.

GEORGE. Everybody back to my place. Come on, all of you. Back to
my place. I'll get a bottle.

*He makes an uncertain way towards the bar as the others get to their
feet.*

16. Exterior. Pub. Night.

*The street's empty except for Carrie and Henry who stand waiting for
George. The pub door is closed, but we hear it being unbolted and George is
let out. He clutches a carrier bag containing bottles.*

GEORGE. Jesus, man, I had a hard time to get this. Lucky the
Guv'nor's a pal of mine. Where are the others? Where's everyone gone?

CARRIE. Buggered off. Never mind them.

She links her arm in George's.

HENRY (*in Afrikaans*). They drove off in their cars.

GEORGE. Gone on ahead, I expect. Okay, we'll walk. We'll catch
them up at my place.

He and Carrie walk off. Henry tags along behind.

17. Interior. Kitchen. Night.

George is stooped in front of the fridge trying to get an ice-tray out. He's impeded by the fact that the fridge hasn't been defrosted for some months and the freezer compartment has become an iceberg of congealed condensation. He's hacking at this mass with a screwdriver, swearing to himself under his breath. Carrie is leaning against the door-jamb holding a bowl in which the ice is to be deposited. Carrie, regarding George, wears a fond smile. She bends forward and, extending a hand, caresses George's head. George, intent on the task in hand, twitches his head irritably. Carrie drops to her knees beside him. She puts an arm round his neck, pulls his head towards her and places her cheek next to his.

CARRIE (*breathily*). George, I feel like it. (*But George has other things on his mind. He continues to chip away at the fridge.*) Oh, George, come on. I *feel* like it.

   George disengages his head and turns to her reprovingly.

GEORGE. Carrie, for God's sake, girl, don't start that now. Here, put down that bowl and go back and talk to him.

CARRIE. I don't fancy 'im.

   George frowns and re-applies himself to his task, jabbing with greater force at the mass of ice.

GEORGE. You not supposed to *fancy* him. You supposed to talk to him. Bring him out of himself.

   Carrie giggles and gets to her feet.

CARRIE. You ask me he hasn't got anything to bring out.

   She turns and walks out. George raises the screwdriver and brings it down with all his strength on the block of ice. With a crash the whole freezer unit detaches itself from its mounting and crashes to the floor. There's a flash from the fridge as it short-circuits and fluid pours out over its contents and the floor of the kitchen. George picks up the frozen mass of metal and carries it over to the sink. He makes room among the debris, lowers the unit under the tap and runs cold water over it.

18. Interior. Living room. Night.

The room has a depraved look. The main lights have been turned out leaving only the twinkle of the Christmas fairy-lights. The inanities of a midnight disc-jockey burble from the radio. Apart from this, and the pop music which succeeds it, there's no sound in the room. George is slumped in the easy chair, Carrie sits at one end of the settee and Henry at the other. There are a number of bottles on the table, beer, wine, and a half bottle of whisky. George levers himself out of his chair, collects a glass from each of the others and, with his own, goes to the table. George inspects each bottle in turn. They're all empty. While this is going on:

CARRIE. A party, you said. Funny sort of party.

GEORGE. I told you to bring your friend for Henry. Why don't you bring your friend if you want a party?

Carrie's silent. After a moment:

CARRIE. Betty won't go with blacks after last time.

George wheels from his inspection of the bottles.

GEORGE. That Betty. Bleddy cold fish.

CARRIE. 'ere we go.

GEORGE. You know something, Henry? These bleddy white girls all the same. Bleddy cold fish, man. Bleddy fillets of plaice.

CARRIE (*confidentially to Henry*). He misses his wife. (*Loudly, to George.*) 'Ere, you gettin' at me by any chance? What the hell you doin', anyway?

GEORGE. We run out of drink, man.

CARRIE. There's a half bottle of gin in me bag.

She leans down and fumbles by the side of the settee and holds out her bag to George. George takes it, opens it and extracts the half bottle, unscrews the top and fills the three glasses. While this is going on:

'E's been tryin' to live dangerously ever since she went off, but he just can't make it. Not but, I mean, he's all right, but he can't seem to enjoy it. (*She pauses, looking for the right phrase.*) What it is, you see. He has regrets. (*She leans over to Henry and whispers.*) 'E won't do it in his wife's bed, you know. He does it in 'ere. Ever so uncomfortable.

George moves away from the table with two glasses which he hands to Henry and Carrie. He goes back for his own.

GEORGE. I'm statin' a fac'. I'm not makin' a racialist statement. I'm statin' a fac'. You' a lovely girl, Carrie, a lovely girl. Not you' fault man. You can't help you' colour.

George shakes his head sadly and sits down, taking extreme care not to spill his glass of gin. After a moment:

CARRIE. Bloody riot this is, innit. Excuse me if I faint from excitement. (*She turns to Henry.*) 'Ere, you wanna dance?

Henry looks at her before replying.

HENRY. I'm sorry, I don't know how to dance to this kind of music.

Carrie rolls her eyes. She drinks her gin. There's a silence. George drinks his gin. He gets up and refills his glass. Carrie holds out hers. George refills her glass, turns to Henry. Henry shakes his head. George walks back to the table to replace the bottle on it. With his back to the other two he lifts the bottle and drains what's left of it. He blinks and gags. He goes back to his seat. The silence persists for a moment. The D.J. on the radio starts to sign off for the night.

CARRIE (*brightly*). 'Ere, what would you do if you 'ad a million pounds? (*Her question elicits no response. She isn't discouraged.*) All right, 'alf a million, then? (*There's still no reply. Even the radio now falls silent.*) You know what I'd do if I 'ad money? First off I'd 'ave plastic surgery. I'd go to the best plastic surgeon in London. That's first off. (*Henry looks at her curiously. Carrie touches her cheek.*) Not for me face, I don't mean. If I 'as money I'd go to a surgeon and get rid of me stretch marks and get me tits done up with plastic and then I'd go for a go-go dancer. (*She turns to Henry.*) I 'ad me first kid at fourteen. I 'ad to own up to it so as to get excused P.E. 'Course, they took me to the court. Care and attention. (*She gives a shrill laugh.*) I never looked back since then. (*She looks across at George.*) In't that right, George? I never looked back. Been ravin' ever since. Ask George. Eh, George?

There's no response from George because George has fallen asleep, his mouth open, his glass, half full, still nursed carefully on his chest. George looks vulnerable. Carrie smiles, then turns to Henry.

They 'ad 'im adopted. I often wonder what happened to the little bugger. They don't tell you, when you sign, see. Well, it might lead to blackmail.

She drinks up her gin, gets to her feet and walks over to George. Carrie carefully disengages his fingers from round his glass, lifts it and empties it. She stands looking down at George.

I'll tell you something about George. 'E's like me, George is. 'E doesn't take advantage. 'E's got principles, George has. 'E could've 'ad ever such a lot of money off that old Canon 'e's always on about. 'E could've 'ad it easy, George could. Like Obed. You met Obed. (*Henry smiles and nods his head*.) Obed works for the Canon. 'E goes round all these countries, Sweden and Denmark and places, raisin' money for the cause. And a bit for himself. 'E doesn't touch what doesn't belong to him. He wouldn't do that. 'E's got very high principles where the cause is concerned. What he does is buy up all that porn and stuff, you know, mags and blue-films, and he flogs it out to South Africa. Oooh, they're mad on it out there. 'E gets it sent out on the diplomatic. I don't know how 'e works it. United Nations or something. George could do that, but he won't. I said to 'im ever so many times, 'George,' I said, 'Why don't you go and get yourself fixed up like Obed.' But he won't. He's got his principles. Of course, Obed's fightin' Apartheid, too. Like he says, he's underminin' their morals. (*Carrie walks and sits down on the settee again.*) Do you know, that Obed, he's got two take-away curry-bars and a self-service launderette. 'Is wives run 'em for 'im. He's got three wives, Obed. (*She's silent for a moment.*) What I mean is, I'm like George. I could 'ave money if I wanted it. I could go on the game. I could go on the game tomorrow. I could make two hundred pound a week on the game. I've thought of it, often. I've got a friend. Liz. My friend Liz is on the game. (*Again, she falls silent. Then, stooping to gather up her purse, she gets to her feet.*) Well, I'm sorry you never had a very nice time. Didn't get goin', really, did it? Oh, well, it's like that, sometimes. Depends on your mood, doesn't it?

Carrie struggles into her coat and moves to the door. Henry gets to his feet.

Well, tara, then. Nice meetin' you. I'll see you again, I expect.

Carrie goes out. Henry follows her to the door.

19. Interior. Corridor. Night.

Carrie is making her way to the stairhead. Henry steps out of the living room into the corridor.

HENRY. Just a moment.

Carrie turns. Henry moves forward. On Carrie's face, briefly, there is an expression of puzzlement. Then, just before it's obscured by Henry, her expression changes. Henry has made his intentions abundantly clear to her. The two dark figures stand for a moment at the stairhead and they move down the corridor to the door of Henry's room. The door's opened and they go inside. From inside the room:

CARRIE. 'Ere! Cor! Oooh, you little bugger ... !

And the door's closed.

20. Interior. Living room. Night.

George is slumped in his chair. He stirs. Without properly waking he stumbles to his feet, gropes behind his chair and drags out his blanket. He picks up the transistor radio from the shelf and lies down on the hearthrug, switching on the transistor. A female voice, distorted by the telephone, describes its symptoms of premenstrual tension. Sympathy is extended by the bright tones of the radio doctor. George snuggles down in his blanket.

21. Interior. Interrogation room. Night.

The voice of the radio doctor changes to the harsh voice of a Special Branch man speaking Afrikaans. There is no set and no indication that we are not still in George's living room. We begin to realise that George has been beaten up. One eye is almost completely closed. His mouth is grotesquely swollen. He is not asleep, but unconscious. The ranting voice is joined by others (Afrikaans). 'Wake the bastard up.' 'Give me the waterhose, Jaanie.' 'You haven't gone and killed the bastard, have you?' etc. etc. A jet of water strikes George in the face. (But the sound is of a lavatory flushing.) George comes to, his head jerking to avoid the jet of water. Hands haul him upright. He's naked, dripping wet. A voice speaks English:

INTERROGATOR. Can't you hear us, boy? You hearing not so good? *(in Afrikaans.)* Put the can on him. *(in English.)* We going to improve you' hearing, you understand me?

Hands bring a four-gallon metal petrol can with one end cut out. Straps are attached to its open end. The can is lowered over George's head. The straps are swiftly buckled under his armpits so the can remains in place. He looks like a mad knight in improvised armour. Hands holding sticks descend on the can, beating it. The noise is intense and it increases. George screams inside the can. The sticks beat on the can with increasing fury. George's screams increase.

22. Interior. Living room. Night.

George is thrashing around in his blanket. The sounds he's making are the strangled yelps of a dreaming dog. The living room door bursts open and Carrie, naked, runs in.

CARRIE. Oh, you poor sod ... *(She runs to George and gets down beside him. She pulls the blanket over herself and snuggles up to him.)* There, George, there ... you poor old sod. Stop it, George, stop it. You're all right, George. Carrie's here, Carrie's with you ...

George's cries subside into moans. His arms go round her. George buries his face in her body. Carrie hugs him, rocking him, stroking his head. George looks up at her.

GEORGE. I had a bleddy horrible nightmare, girl. Bleddy horrible ...

CARRIE. All right, George. Go to sleep now. I'll stay with you.

He smiles up at her.

23. Interior. Stairs and landing. Day.

Zazie is climbing the stairs. She carries a suitcase. Behind her comes her eldest daughter, Chloe. Jason brings up the rear. Chloe's a very pretty girl in her mid-twenties, very clean and neat. She wears jeans and a T-shirt with a jacket. Zazie stops at the top of the stairs to get her breath back. Chloe walks past her into the kitchen. Jason hangs onto the gate at the stairtop. Chloe looks round the kitchen and turns back to her mother.

CHLOE. My God, Mam, it looks like a bomb went off in here.

ZAZIE. He's helpless, that man. Make a start, anyway.

Zazie walks down the corridor towards the living room but, instead of going in, opens the door next to it, the marital bedroom. She goes in.

24. Interior. Bedroom. Day.

Zazie enters. The room is semi-darkness, the curtains drawn. She walks across and pulls them back. The room is in the state which she left it, untouched by human hand. The furnishings are similar to those of the rest of the flat, somewhat florid and somewhat lavish, quilted satin bedhead, a teasmade beside the bed, dressing-table with flounces, embossed frame round the mirror. Zazie takes off her coat and throws it on the satin bedspread. On her way back to the door she runs a finger over the dressing-table surface. It's thick with dust. She goes out.

25. Interior. Landing and corridor. Day.

Zazie comes out of the bedroom. She calls to Chloe in the kitchen.

ZAZIE. He's gone back to sleepin' on the floor.

> *She opens the door of the living room and goes in. Jason steals along the passage towards the living room. He puts his head round the open door. Zazie, coming out again, collides with him. She puts out a hand to steady him. She speaks to him mildly.*

Go down you' own part of the house, Jason.

> *Zazie pushes Jason aside and walks down the passage to the kitchen. She stands at the kitchen door.*

Come along Chloe, you can leave it.

26. Interior. Kitchen. Day.

Chloe has an apron on and she's been clearing a place in the sink to start the washing up. Dishes and pots are piled in an unstable pyramid on the draining board. Chloe looks round at her mother. Chloe takes off her apron. Her mother disappears into the bedroom.

27. Interior. Stairs and corridor. Day.

Chloe comes out of the kitchen with her jacket on. Zazie comes out of the bedroom with her coat on, carrying the suitcase. She closes the door carefully. She walks towards Chloe who waits at the head of the stairs. The door facing them at the far end of the corridor opens and Henry appears. He's naked except for his shirt. Zazie and Chloe regard him unemotionally. They start to descend the stairs. Henry ducks back into his room, closing the door. The heads of Zazie and Chloe disappear from view down the stairs. Jason, who has been hanging about in the corridor, runs into the kitchen. There's a crash. The dishes cascade across the kitchen floor and spill out onto the landing. He runs out and disappears down the stairs.

28. Interior. Living room. Day.

Henry sits alone on the sofa. Carrie sits at the table nibbling at a packet of crisps left over from last night. George is slumped in his fireside chair. There's an atmosphere of gloomy post-mortem. Carrie, after a silence, looks up.

CARRIE. I'll tell you one thing, George. If he goes, I go.

GEORGE. All right. That's all right by me. You can go any time. Who asked you to stay, anyway.

Carrie placidly munches a crisp and speaks matter-of-factly:

CARRIE. Grateful little pig you are, aren't you?

Carrie looks round her.

GEORGE. He told the Canon he was a victim of apartheid ... (*Henry makes a protesting sound. George glares at him and he falls silent.*) And now it comes out that all that's wrong with him, he's had a nervous breakdown.

He gives a contemptuous snort. Carrie bridles.

CARRIE. How d'you think he got it, then? You don't just get a nervous breakdown from just nothing at all, do you?

GEORGE. You don't get it from the SBs either. You get your head bashed in, and you get hung up by your thumbs and you get your prick nailed to a table but you don't get a bloody nervous breakdown, I can tell you. They keep you too bloody busy for you to think about nervous breakdowns.

CARRIE. Oh, shut up, George. Tell him, Henry. Go on. Tell him how you got your nervous breakdown then. (*Henry looks shyly away.*) Go on. What you worried about? Tell him.

Henry starts to mutter in Afrikaans. The mutter gradually becomes louder and more distinct. It grows in volume and urgency until it becomes a flood. Henry's excitement increases. He jumps to his feet and addresses George, drowning him in a spate of Afrikaaner indignation, arms flailing. Finally he runs out of steam. His voice falters, an expression of panic comes over his face. He turns and sits down on the

sofa again, looking down at his hands, twisting his fingers nervously
together. There's a silence. George is inspecting the carpet at his feet.
Carrie's staring at Henry, awestricken. At length, almost in a whisper:

What's he say?

George doesn't at first reply. After a moment he speaks grudgingly:

GEORGE. He got his nervous breakdown trying not to get arrested.

Carrie looks at Henry in complete bewilderment. She gets up and sits
beside him on the sofa. She takes his hands in hers and looks earnestly
into his face.

CARRIE. You don't want to worry just because nothing every
happened to you. George never meant nothing. What it is, if you
haven't had done to you what George had done to him he doesn't think
you're one with him, see.

Carrie smiles at him with kindness, like a student nurse with a geriatric.

See what I mean?

He raises his head and gives her an answering smile.

GEORGE. He's a Doctor of Philosophy.

CARRIE. He's what?

GEORGE. He's a bloody professor.

Carrie stares at Henry, impressed. Henry tries to look blameless.

CARRIE. Cor!

George gets to his feet and walks to the door.

Where you going?

GEORGE. Out.

And he does so.

29. Interior. Bedroom. Day.

George has the wardrobe open, he has taken out his smart suit and laid it on the bed. He's now engaged in taking off his clothes. He's down to socks and underpants as Carrie enters. Carrie watches as he looks through his chest of drawers for a reasonably respectable shirt. He finds a moderately clean shirt and slips it on. Carrie regards him with a jaundiced eye.

CARRIE. You treat people like shit, George. You know that? You treat people like shit.

She stares at him malevolently. He takes no notice, pulling on his trousers.

Jealous. You're bleedin' jealous. Green with it. Jealous of that poor sod because he's a doctor of whatsit and you're only a bloody brickie. You can't stand it because he's a proper professor and you're nothing but a bleedin' labourer. All right, you done a bit of time out there and he never. That don't mean nothin'. All that means he's got enough bleedin' nous not to get caught. For all you know he might've done a murder. What call've you got to go layin' down the law? I'll tell you one thing, you're not layin' down no law on ...

Carrie breaks off. George is advancing on her. He's let go his trousers and they've dropped round his ankles, turning his progress into a shambling shuffle, but no less menacing for that. She gives a shriek and backs away. He brings back his hand and lets her have it across the side of her head. She falls sideways onto the bed. He stands looking down at her. She whimpers. He stoops and pulls up his trousers, walks away and starts threading his belt through the loops as if nothing had happened. Carrie looks at him warily, then sits up. She shakes her head and rubs it with one hand. She sighs.

All right. I'm sorry. The day I learn to keep me mouth shut and me legs crossed ...

George is knotting his tie, he glances at her. Then he opens a drawer, rifles about under the clothes and pulls out a large square photograph, a group photograph, mounted on card. He takes it over to the bed and shows it to Carrie. The photograph. It shows a gathering of civic dignitaries, men and women, a po-faced lot, middle-aged and middle-

class whites, with, a jewel of grinning pride in a sombre assembly,
George.

(*Exclaiming.*) George, it's you!

GEORGE. Urban District Councillor. (*He sits down on the bed beside
her.*) Unfortunately, after I made my first public speech I was arrested.
Two years I was on the Council and every time I open my mouth they
put me in gaol. Zazie never knew whether I was comin' home or
whether she got to go down the police station to see if I was picked up
again. When I was arrested Zazie would go round the Black Sash ladies
and they'd give her the money to pay my admission of guilt fine and
they'd turn me loose again. Up until last time, that is, when the bastards
picked me up with a bag of explosives right outside the police station. I
wasn't going to blow the police station, I was going to blow the Pass
Office, but they wouldn't believe that.

*He takes the picture from her and replaces it under the clothing in the
drawer. Then he turns and looks at her, leaning on the chest of drawers.*

Those people I was on the Council with, good people, Liberal
people, when I got out of detention, when they sprung me out of
Robben Island, they fixed it so I got a franchise. That mean I get to
run a store, a store in the township. Of course, I couldn't run the store
because I was under house arrest and banning order. Zazie ran the
store. Zazie and her cousin and her uncle and her brother-in-law and
his wife, they run the store and I used to sit out back, drinking beer
and smoking cigarettes. Those stores, they gold mines. The people got
to come to your store or they got to go one mile, maybe two mile to
the next store. And the next store just the same as yours. All the
people in the township come to your store. And you buy jam, seven
pound tin of jam and you sell that jam two spoonful at a time. A tikky
– that's threepence – for a spoonful. Same with tea and sugar and
flour. All those things you sell. Whatever you want to sell you make
money on. Zazie workin' day and night. She hearin' that bell ringin' on
that till and it sound in her ear like the chimes of Christmas. Zazie
buys herself some nice dresses, my kids are going for piano lessons, my
brother-in-law buys himself a car and Zazie's Uncle's betting on
horses. We a happy family. The sun is shining on us and I sit all day
in my chair drinking beer and later on I drink wine and brandy and
sometimes I drink a bottle of Van der Hum just like bloody

Commissioner Steenkamp drink. (*He stands smiling at her.*)
Unfortunately ...

> *Carrie gets up off the bed and goes to him. She lays her head on his chest. He strokes her hair, smiling.*

30. Interior. Reception suite.

A reception is in progress. The guests are colourfully dressed and of many races, Indians, Africans, Chinese, Malaysians and Middle-Easterns with a sprinkling of patrician whites. Suits are smart, dresses are wafty and there are tribal robes and ethnic headgear. Food and drink is being served by well-spoken and well-nourished daughters and wives of the Movement. George can be seen next to the drinks table on which are ranked bottles of champagne. He's talking animatedly to an elegant Indian of effeminate appearance wearing a Parsee hat. Modwe and Obed are also present. Sandra stands just inside the door, welcoming arrivals. The Canon enters with his companion.

CANON. Ah, Sandra, my dear, how nice, how very nice. You know Dame Elspeth?

> *The Canon turns to make the introduction but Dame Elspeth has steamed past him, arms outstretched, cooing like a dove, towards a gigantic Sikh. The Canon frowns.*

Dreadful woman. But bloody rich.

> *He grins boyishly. A pretty girl offers him a tray and he takes a glass of champagne. He twinkles at the girl.*

I say, this is *very* nice, *very*.

> *The girl twinkles back.*

SANDRA. We decided to do the catering ourselves. We weren't having slave labour at a function like this.

CANON. Quite, quite ...

> *The Canon, sipping his champagne, has his eyes on an even prettier girl offering canapés. He smiles vaguely at Sandra, and moves off in the*

wake of the girl, bowing to delegates as they recognise him. George spots him across the room and pushes through the crowd. He breaks in on the Canon's conversation with the girl with the canapés. He stuffs a canapé into his mouth and beams at her. She's delightedly confused. The Canon turns to George.

George, my dear fellow! And how's young whatsisname? Settling down, is he?

GEORGE. First class, Canon. He's coming along fine. (*He leans forward conspiratorially.*) Canon, you saw the fellow I was speaking with over there?

The Canon becomes wary.

CANON. No. Can't say I did, George.

GEORGE. It so happens that when that fellow was in Moscow he got in a bit of hot water with the authorities. They kept it quiet at the time because of the other party involved. Of course, he doesn't suspect that I know anything, but if you were to give me the word ...

He gives the Canon a knowing wink. The Canon recalls:

CANON. George, honestly, you must try to be more discreet. They are very influential people here.

George laughs.

GEORGE. Don't worry, Canon. I know how to keep my trap shut. (*He nods mysteriously and starts to move away. But he turns.*) Canon, remember. The time for speaking is past. Remember that.

And he moves off. The Canon looks anxiously round and spots Mokwe. He moves towards him.

CANON. Mokwe, old chap.

MOKWE. Canon! This is a real pleasure! What do you think? A good attendance, eh?

CANON. Splendid, splendid. You've done a great job, as usual. Mokwe, I was wondering, will George be addressing the Conference?

MOKWE. Oh, yes, Canon. He looks forward to this the whole year.

Tomorrow will be his big day. He's the last speaker before the lunch break, just like last year.

CANON. Do you happen to know what he'll be speaking on?

MOKWE. As in previous years. The South African Police and Security System. His special subject. He's a very forceful speaker on that subject. His description of Police methods and of detention on Robben Island is very vivid. All the Delegates enjoy George's address.

CANON. Good, good. As lóng as it's nothing too controversial.

They turn to look for George. He's at the door. Catching Mokwe's eye he raises a hand in a surreptitious farewell and slips out of the door. He carries his briefcase. It seems more than usually bulky.

31. Interior. George's living room. Night.

The lights are turned on as George enters. He goes to the table and opens his briefcase. He takes out a bottle of champagne which he places on the table. He then takes off his overcoat, throws it on the settee and lights the gas fire. He takes down the transistor and switches it on. Classical music. Then he goes back to the table and uncorks the champagne. The cork pops satisfyingly, the wine fizzes. He pours himself a glass. Carrie enters. She wears only Henry's greatcoat. It totally envelopes her.

CARRIE. Hello, George. Have a good time, did you? Ooh, champagne. You nick that, did you?

GEORGE. It's kosher.

He pours her a glassful.

CARRIE. It's what?

He shows her the bottle.

GEORGE. Mount Carmel Sparkling White. Sandra had it left over from her nephew's Bar Mitzvah. They had to wrap it up in napkins in case the Arabs spotted it.

CARRIE. Arabs don't drink.

GEORGE. Progressive Arabs do.

CARRIE. You're havin' me on. I know they don't because I had a Lebanese and that's Arab and he never touched it.

George picks up the bottle and walks over to the easy chair. George plops down in it and pulls off his tie, stretches his legs out.

My feller was on pills. Dreadful, he was. Wouldn't let you alone. Worse 'n him in there. (*She jerks her head towards the door.*) 'Course it couldn've been the eggnog. Lived on eggnog, he did.

She walks over and perches on the arm of George's chair. They sip their drinks in silence for a moment.

George, you ever wonder what's going to happen to us? (*He glances up at her.*) No, I mean, you know how people are always lookin' out for things to get better and better? (*She pauses and frowns.*) It doesn't seem to me that things get better and better. (*Another pause while she thinks how to express herself.*) I'm not saying things get worse, not necessarily. But I can't see things get better. Know what I mean?

She finishes her drink and holds out her glass. George refills it.

I mean, say you go round thinking things are gettin' better, like people do. And say it *looks* as though things are getting better. Then, when you think they *have* got better you turn round and ... and well, it seems like they haven't after all. (*She pauses and thinks very hard indeed. Then:*) George. Eggnog's alcoholic, isn't it?

George doesn't answer. She looks down at him, then allows her body to slip down the inside of the arm so she's crowding him in the chair. Carrie puts her free arm along the back of the chair, resting on his shoulders and lays her cheek on his head.

George ... I been thinkin'. What if I was to move in here permanent.

George moves, dislodging her head. He looks up at her. Her tone has a hint of wheedling in it. He grins at her. She affects annoyance.

Oh, George! I done *him* a bit o' good didn't I? He's cheered up lovely. Well, it's what you wanted, wasn't it? Get him on his feet? (*She giggles then she frowns.*) No, I'm serious, George. Like, with me and the two of you, it wouldn't get so bleedin' 'eavy. See what I mean? I mean, with the both of you, I wouldn't feel I got to be soddin' happy and cheerful all the bloody time. Like you do when you're with just one feller. (*She adds.*) Not but what I don't like a laugh. I do. I like a bit of a laugh. What you think? What you say, George? If I was to move in permanent?

GEORGE. Yes. All right, Carrie. If you want. You do what you want, Carrie.

She leans forwards and kisses the top of his head.

CARRIE. Oooh, lovely. I'll fetch me things tomorrow. (*She jumps up and drains her glass. She moves to the table and puts it down. She's about to go but:*) 'Ere, George, you're not pissed off, are you?

George looks across at her and smiles.

GEORGE. No. No, I'm not pissed off.

CARRIE. 'Cause if you was ... I mean, I don't mind bunkin' down here.

GEORGE. No. I'm tired, that's all. Those bleddy receptions Sandra gives. Tirin'. Like you say, you got to be happy and cheerful all the time. Tires you out, man. And tomorrow I got to make my bleddy speech.

CARRIE. All right. I'll let you get a bit of kip, then. G'night.

GEORGE. Goodnight, Carrie.

She goes. He remains seated in his chair. Gradually the hand holding the glass drops. His eyes close. He sleeps.

32. Interior. Interrogation room. Night.

George has been strapped to a wooden frame. He's naked. From one of his ears, from his fingers, from his penis, from one of his nipples, wires, attached to his body by alligator clips, run to a bench on which is a black box and brass terminals and a handle. Hands steady the box and hold the handle. The handle starts to turn. Slowly at first, then more rapidly. George quivers, then as the current increases, jerks convulsively. His convulsions increase and the alligator clips jumps off his earlobe. A voice shouts:

VOICE. The bleddy clips fallin' off. Can't you put the clips on right, man?

The hand on the machine stops turning and another voice answers.

SECOND VOICE. He got too many clips on him.

FIRST VOICE. Stick one up his arse, then.

SECOND VOICE. He got one up his arse. He got an electrode up his arse.

A mutter from first voice. The hand starts turning the handle again. On George's face, sweating, twitching. He's trying to speak. A strange sound comes from his mouth, convulsed by the shocks.

GEORGE. Praat, praat, praat. Ik vil praat ... Talk ... I talk ... talk, talk, talk, talk, talk, talk.

33. Interior. Living room. Night.

George is stretched out straight, stiff, twitching. He's making a sound.

GEORGE. Tok, tok, tok, tok ... tok ... tok ...

And opens his eyes. As he wakens he relaxes. He heaves himself out of the chair, fetches out his blanket from behind it, wraps himself in it, lies down on the hearthrug before the fire. He stretches out a hand and pulls the transistor nearer to him. He sighs and rolls over, closing his eyes again. There's a small smile on his face.

34. Exterior. Commonwealth Institute. Day.

Mokwe can be seen standing outside the main entrance to the Institute. Up the path leading to the Institute the Delegates to the Commonwealth Anti-Apartheid League are moving, not in one group, but strolling in twos and threes. Only one or two are white, the rest of the party consists of turbanned Indians, Malaysians, Chinese, Africans in robes or in smart suits, and Arabs in tribal dress or headgear. They pass into the building, nodding to Mokwe, who appears distracted. Mokwe, alone looks left and right, glancing at his watch. At last George appears. Mokwe hurries forward to meet him and escorts him into the building.

MOKWE (*off*). He's bringing the movement into dispute, that's what he's doing ...

35. Interior. Living room. Sandra's mansion flat.

Evidence of South Africa in the decor. Brownish watery lithographs of stylised springboks, etc. Books in shelves show literacy inclination of owner. Feathery grasses in tall earthware jars, leather pouffes with arabic inscriptions. Mokwe stands in the centre of his scandalised friends, those we met in the pub, plus Zazie and Lily.

MOKWE. From all over the Commonwealth they comin'. Some of those men riskin' their lives to attend this Conference and he's tellin' them jokes. He supposed to speak on the South African Police and Security System, and he's telling jokes.

OBED. What kind of jokes, man?

MOKWE. Jokes about the progress we makin' in the movement. In this country.

SANDRA. Jokes against *us*, you mean?

Everyone looks grave.

MOKWE. Jokes about how the South African Government giving itself a medal for thirty years in office. He reading it out of the paper, man, how that's a world record of any Government for stability in office. How that medal goin' to have John Vorster's head on one side and his cock on the other.

Obed smothers a laugh. Sandra's indignant.

SANDRA. That can't be true, can it? John Vorster's head on one side and his ... thing on the other?

MOKWE. Of course not, Sandra, that's his joke. They going to put a

kruithoring on it, a powderhorn. The Nationalist Party Emblem.
George says that's John Vorster's cock. That's his joke. And he makes
jokes about the deaths in Police detention.

SANDRA. Oh, I say! That's truly bad taste.

MOKWE. Yes, bad taste. Very bad taste. He says that John Vorster
announce that deaths in Police detention greatly exaggerated. He say
that means those people not as dead as they reported. He say the
people die in Police detention today don't get so death like they used
to. Only a little bit dead. He say that shows how we makin' progress.
Then he says that when they hung him out the window in John
Vorster Square Police Station they hung him out the fifteenth floor.
Nowadays they hang people out the tenth floor. He says that's an
improvement of five floors. That's the kind of joke he's making. Jokes
about the progress of the Movement. In this country.

Sandra's clearly very distressed.

SANDRA. Well!

Obed smiles.

OBED. George is a bit headstrong. I tell you, man, if his clock-timer
hadn't ticked so loud he'd have blown the Police Station and every
bugger in it.

MOKWE. That was a mistake. He miss his way. He says he was
picked up *outside* the Police Station.

OBED. Outside the Police Station, yes. Outside the yard trying to
push his bag through the window with a bamboo cane. That was no
mistake, man.

SANDRA. Exactly! You're saying that George is irresponsible, aren't
you?

MOKWE. He like that explosive, man. He like the bang, the big bang.
I like it too. When you light that fuse and you wait, it all dark and you
tremblin' and waitin' and then it come. Bang! Whoosh! And you
runnin'. Runnin' and laughin'! Oh, man, that make you feel good.

OBED. George is missin' that. He got a lot of fight in him, man, and
he got nothin' to fight. That's George's trouble. He still want to go on
fightin'.

Lily glares at them disapprovingly.

SANDRA. We all want to go on fighting, I hope. But most of us have managed to put the past behind us and settled down and got jobs. I mean we do have to accept the realities of our situation don't we?

There's a silence. Sandra's reminder of their situation is unwelcome.

BILLIE. He wants to go back to South Africa. He's always talking about it. Why don't we club together and see if we can't....

Sandra interrupts.

SANDRA. Billie, darling, that just shows how out of touch with us you are. None of us can ever go back. You ought to know that.

BILLIE. I thought you went back last year.

SANDRA. That was entirely different. Ma died and there was property to dispose of. And I only managed that because of ... well, anyway, I was truly lucky to get out again, I can tell you.

BILLIE (*sarcastically*). I didn't mean send him off on an ASS flight to Jo'burg or something. I meant if we got him out to Mozambique or somewhere they'd ... they'd what you call it, infiltrate him.

OBED. George knows as well as I know that's just not feasible for a man with his record. The Liberation Movement got enough troubles of their own without men like George and me. You send George out there to those Liberation Movement people and they put him in the suicide squad or they sell him over to the SBs for one of their own people. Nobody sees George no more, believe me.

Everyone regards each other warily. There's a feeling that never seeing George again might be a solution. Sandra banishes the thought for him.

SANDRA. Look, we have to put our personal feelings aside. We really can't let George go on like this. For his own good, I mean. We have to think of poor old George and what's best for him. One of us has simply got to take him in hand.

There's a lack of volunteers. Somehow attention is turned towards Zazie. Zazie looks round at them defensively. Lily comes to her rescue.

LILY. Everybody talking about George. What's best for George. What we going to do for George. Got to think of George. Who is thinking about Zazie?

Zazie's a little embarrassed. She mutters:

ZAZIE. George has got principles. That's the trouble with that man. Principles. (*She smiles and shakes her head.*) When he released from detention, we get that store, and what he do? He steal from the store. He's stealin' out of his own store and givin' the things away to the people out at the back. More people goin' to the back of the store for free than comin' to the front and payin'. That's his principle, he say.

LILY. We all got principles, man, but that George is not the same as we. That George is crazy, man.

SANDRA. George can be difficult, I think we'd all say that. But that's why he needs help. Zazie, I know you've had a hard time, but won't you give him one more chance?

Zazie's indignation bubbles over:

ZAZIE. You sayin' I got to take him in my new clean flat?

Sandra glances round at the others uncertainly.

SANDRA. I think we are saying that, aren't we?

Zazie draws herself up.

ZAZIE. When he behavin' bad before, when he causin' trouble and anxiety to your movement, what you tellin' me? (*She glares round them. They make no response.*) You tellin' me to leave him. You tellin' me to walk out on him. Make him see the consequences of his actions. That's what you tellin' me.

SANDRA. Oh, no, Zazie, I beg your pardon, I never said that. I merely pointed out that he was being very irresponsible and getting himself talked about and that you owed it to yourself and to all of us to take him in hand. I *never* suggested you should leave him.

ZAZIE. You tellin' me that George livin' a bad life, that George not a good husband for me. The house always full of people, full of drinkin', full of talk, talk, talk. Very well, I listen to you and I think you're speaking truly and I walk out of that place and I leave him alone with those people and I tell him I will not return except he become a proper husband to me. Now you tellin' me to go back, now when he worse than even before, with women and the house broken up and dirty, dirty, and more people in there, and ... and ... No! No, I will not go back. I got a nice life for myself. Me and my Chloe. Yes, I miss him. I miss him with his talk, talk, talk and his bad ways, and his crazy principles. Well, I got my principles as well. And my principles is not to go back nursing on the bleddy National Health carrying bedpans and washing sluice. My principle is to carry on with my private patient nursing, that the first principle. That good money and easy work. Just to sit and see they dying quietly. That's good work for a woman like me. That my first principle. And my second principle is the house be clean. And my third principle is there be no women in that house, no women and no men either. And my last principle is George come to me and tell me he want me to come back to him. That's my principles, man, and if I don't get my principles he don't get me back. (*She walks to the door. Here she turns and faces them.*) But he won't do that. I know him. He don't give in easy, George don't. He don't give in. (*She stares round at them, her eyes filling with tears.*) I don't want him ... I don't want him to give in. I don't want ...

> *Zazie can't finish what she wants to say. She turns, scrabbles at the door knob and goes out. Her footsteps echo along the passage. We hear the hollow slam of the front door of the flat. Lily jumps up and follows her out. Everyone looks accusingly at Sandra. Sandra bridles. No one says anything. Sandra tries again.*

SANDRA. I can't imagine why she should have taken it all so personally. I was only thinking of the effect of George's behaviour on the good name of the Movement. (*She looks round and catches Billie's eye on her.*) I suppose it is hard for anyone who hasn't been through what we've been through to understand our feelings when one of us starts backsliding.

BILLIE. I've never really understood what it was you did go through, Sandra.

> *Sandra glares at her. Mokwe seeks to save embarrassment.*

MOKWE. George is enjoying himself, man. He livin' in that place with Henry and that Carrie, he happy as a pig in shit man.

> *Obed starts to laugh, quelled by a look from Sandra.*

SANDRA. I don't think it's funny. We've got to do something. (*No one has any suggestions.*) Is that girl supporting him? (*No one answers.*) I mean, what's he living on?

MOKWE. He's speaking at Colleges. They pay him a few pound for that. And he got his book. He put a lot on selling his book when that finished.

SANDRA. That's not an income.

Mokwe laughs.

SANDRA. If he was made to face the fact that he's got to earn a living like anyone else – which he's perfectly capable of doing – he'll buckle down and get a job. And once he's working regularly he won't have time to ... I mean it'll use up some of that surplus energy of his, won't it? And besides, it'll bring him more into contact with ordinary normal people.

BILLIE. How are you proposing to do that? Starve him out? Very nice.

SANDRA. Of course not. It's perfectly simple. I'll speak to the Canon. He'll have to make some other arrangement for Henry. I don't think the girl's a problem. Of course, I've no doubt that he owes oodles of back rent, but I'll have a word with Mr Korsciuski. Once he knows we're taking a personal interest I'm sure he'll be sympathetic. And then, as soon as we've got George's personal life sorted out we can ... well, we can start to apply a bit of pressure.

Obed gives a shout of laughter.

OBED. Hell, Sandra, you applying sanctions to George. Let's hope it work on him better than it work on old Vorster.

BILLIE. Let's hope it works better than it did on Zazie. If Sandra shows her usual degree of tact and understanding poor old George could find himself out on the street.

36. Exterior. George's house. Day.

First floor front window. Jason's grubby person. He's smearing the glass with jammy fingers, grinning. Below on the pavement side of the fence is stacked the contents of the flat. On the settee sit George and Henry with Carrie between them. Of the three only George appears relaxed. They sit in silence for a moment. Then:

CARRIE. How d'you know they'll rehouse you.

GEORGE. When you evicted they got to rehouse you. It's in the act. They got no choice, man. I tell you, he done me a real favour, evictin' me. Now I'll get a real nice place on the Council, on one of them estates. You see. He done me a real favour.

A furniture removal van arrives.

37. Exterior. Street. Day.

A street of Bed and Breakfast hotels of the kind one finds around King's Cross. Mokwe is walking down the street glancing up at the hotels as he passes them, consulting a paper he holds in his hand. He enters one of the hotels.

38. Interior. George's Room. Day.

A long narrow room partitioned off from a larger room. A wash-basin in one corner with a mirror over it, a dressing-table before the window with no mirror over it, a bed, bedside table. George sits before the dressing-table on a straight-back chair. He's thoroughly preoccupied, measuring out powder from a packet of proprietary weedkiller onto one of the pans of an old-fashioned set of letter-scales. On the dressing-table top lies a book, entitled 'S.O.E. The Official History of Clandestine Operations in Europe, 1939–1945', A chemist's packet labelled 'Permanganate of Potash', another labelled 'Aluminium Powder', a packet of Tate and Lyle's icing sugar, a packet of french letters, one of which has been unrolled, a small pudding bowl and a wooden spoon. George completes his weighing out of the powder and puts it in the mixing bowl. He stirs the bowl. He picks up a funnel and places the thin end into the end of the french letter. He pours the contents of the pudding bowl into the funnel and shakes the powder down into the french letter. Over all this we hear the footsteps of Mokwe climbing the stairs, slackening as he gains height and fatigue tells. The footsteps stop outside George's door and only then does George look up. He listens. Outside Mokwe knocks on the wrong door. George remains tense. Mokwe knocks again on the wrong door, then, getting no answer, he knocks on George's door. George leaps into action, whipping a towel from the rail beside the basin and covering the surface of the dressing-table with it. He goes to the door, unlocks it and opens it cautiously. Seeing Mokwe he opens it, retreating before him into the bedroom. Mokwe looks round curiously. George regards him in silence. At length Mokwe turns to him.

MOKWE. Well, George ... (*George nods, smiling.*) You difficult to track down, Man.

GEORGE. They rehouse me.

MOKWE. Yes. That's how I found you. The Social Security told me.

GEORGE. Bed and Breakfast. Forty-two pound a week they payin' out for me here.

Mokwe moves to the window and looks out. George sits down on the bed. Mokwe turns from the window, twitches George's chair and sits down.

MOKWE. Lily been after me.

GEORGE. I gone underground, man. I had eight hundred pound phone bill at that place.

MOKWE. Canon paid that for you. (*George looks guilty.*) And your back rent. And the electric. All paid. (*George looks hang-dog.*) And he got a job for you. (*George shakes his head miserably and looks down at his knees.*) He goin' to fix you up with a mini cab. (*George looks up.*) They got a fund. Rehabilitation Fund. They buy you a mini-cab. Your own business. You pay them back when you able. That's not a charity, man. You your own boss.

GEORGE. I can't drive.

MOKWE. You got no licence? (*George shakes his head.*) You better start to learn. You speak to the Canon. He fix you up with a driving school. This is your chance, man. (*But George is shaking his head. Mokwe looks at him suspiciously.*) You livin' here on your own?

George nods. He grins.

GEORGE. Carrie gone on the game with her friend Liz.

MOKWE. And that fellow Henry? What happened to him?

GEORGE. He's just popped out for a minute. He's gone round to the public library.

MOKWE. And what you doin', man?

George looks furtive, glancing towards the dressing-table. Mokwe shifts his chair to look and it knocks against the dressing-table, dislodging one of the packets under the towel. A thin stream of shining powder dribbles onto the floor. Mokwe looks down at it, then stretches out a hand and dabbles a finger in it. He examines his finger tip.

MOKWE. Aluminium powder. What in hell you doin', man?

GEORGE. Decoratin'. Bit of home decoratin'. Cheer the place up a bit.

Mokwe stares at him suspiciously, gets up and whips off the towel. He looks down at the materials on the dressing-table top. He picks up the french letter.

MOKWE. Shit, man, you using that old potassium chlorate igniter?

GEORGE. What's wrong with that? You get a good flash with that.

MOKWE. What your charge?

GEORGE. Plastic. It's in the book, there.

He walks over and shows Mokwe. Mokwe glances down the page.

MOKWE. Jesus, this is a useful book, man. 'History of Special Operations.' This is official book, man. Where you get this book—!

GEORGE. Public Library.

Mokwe nods and puts the book down.

MOKWE. Still, that Pot Chlor no good for you. You need to use Ammonal in between the igniter and the charge so you get acceleration.

Mokwe stares at him. Then he looks round at the mess of chemicals on

the table. George looks at him stubbornly. Mokwe, coming to a decision,
moves quickly to the door.

Wait here. Don't you move. Don't you touch that stuff. You wait
for me.

And he dives out of the door. George looks after him, then seats himself
at the dressing-table. He opens the top drawer and takes out a plastic
container of liquid. It's labelled 'battery acid'.

39. Interior. Hotel landing. Day.

Mokwe is on the pay phone. He presses a two-pence piece into the slot as
he hears the bleep-bleep-bleep.

MOKWE. Obed ... Obed, man, it's Mokwe. Listen, you got to come
round here ... No, no ... it's George. I'm at ...

But he gets no further. There's a dull rumble from upstairs which grows
into a sizeable explosion. Plaster falls from the ceiling in a cloud. The
explosion's followed by the crackle of flames.

40. Interior. Landing. Hotel. Day.

The landing outside George's room. His door has been blown out and hangs
by broken hinges. Smoke billows out from the open doorway. The flicker of
flames can be seen. From this inferno the blackened form of George
appears, groping its way towards the landing. His face wears an expression
of puzzlement. Over this we hear the sound of police syrens, fire engine
bells, the screech of tyres on tarmac.

41. Exterior. Hospital. Day.

There is nothing to indicate that this is not an ordinary hospital. Sandra
leads the way from Car Park to Wards. Zazie, Lily and Mokwe follow.
They enter one of the buildings.

42. Interior. Mental hospital. Corridor.

The small procession walk along the corridor. A nameplate on the wall directs them to: Cecil Rhodes Ward.

43. Interior. Day ward. Day.

A large room resembling a recreation room. There's a TV set, a table-tennis table, a pool table, easy chairs set round low tables and straight chairs set round high ones. It's all a bit shabby, however, and the atmosphere is bleak. Patients, sitting or wandering about, one staring fixedly out of the window, are mostly clothed, dressed with the lack of care of people with nowhere to go. Others wear hospital pyjamas and dressing gowns. Nasri, an Indian male Charge-Nurse, lounges against the chair of a patient who, with three or four others is watching 'Hyn o Fyd' on TV. A couple of white-coated doctors, making their rounds, have stopped to watch a game of draughts. Neither of the two players has made a move for some time. Their immobility is complete. One of the doctors, a young Indian woman, Doctor Bannerjee, leans forward, and with a smile, makes a move for one of the players. The second player fixes her with an outraged glare and sweeps board and draughtsmen onto the floor. Nasri appears beside the second Doctor, Fitzpatrick, a healthy-looking man in his late thirties, and indicates Sandra and her group who are standing just inside the door. He accompanies Fitzpatrick towards them while we stay on the draughtsplayer, who, Doctor Bannerjee having administered a gentle admonition, has sunk to his knees on the floor and is gathering up the scattered draughtsmen. Doctor Bannerjee is crouching beside him to help. Doctor Fitzpatrick has joined Sandra. Nasri has returned to the TV set.

SANDRA. *Melancholia?*

FITZPATRICK. Melancholia, yes. The old terminology was rather daunting. George is just a bit depressed.

A puzzled silence.

ZAZIE. But what's the *matter* with him?

FITZPATRICK. Oh, nothing complicated. Straightforward clinical depression.

This is yet more disconcerting. Sandra suddenly gets it.

SANDRA. This is a *mental* hospital!

Zazie, in particular, shows extreme distress. Fitzpatrick, seeing this, places a comforting hand on her arm.

FITZPATRICK. Let's all sit down for a moment, shall we?

He shepherds them to a circle of easy chairs. As they go:

FITZPATRICK. George has been having a bit of a rough time. Things rather piling up on him ...

Doctor Bannerjee joins them as they sit. She stands beside Fitzpatrick's chair.

FITZPATRICK. ... and when that happens, things getting a bit too much to cope with, chap can't seem to see a way out, this wretched depression sets in.

Lily looks at Zazie. Her voice is doom-laden.

LILY. What I told you, Zazie? What I say to you? And now look what happens. He gone out of his mind.

Zazie's face puckers. She turns her head away. Fitzpatrick pats her knee.

FITZPATRICK. Now, now, now. There's really nothing to worry about. Your husband isn't a mental case in the strict sense. Clinical depression is a physiological disorder. It's just as if he was suffering from hypertension or a stomach ulcer. Just like an ulcer. Treatable.

SANDRA. He's certainly had plenty to be depressed about. (*She turns to the others.*) I'm sure we never thought for one moment that Mr Korsciuski would ...

FITZPATRICK. No, no. That's quite a different kind of depression. That's what happens when you've had a row with your boyfriend or your dear old mother's been run over by a bus. Something you get over fairly easily. George has *clinical* depression. Something you don't get over without a bit of help. Fortunately we're able to treat it with a reasonable degree of success.

Sandra is becoming increasingly suspicious. Fitzpatrick smiles at her reassuringly.

FITZPATRICK. We've got George on a mild tranquilliser and a course of ECT.

SANDRA. ECT!

Zazie leans towards her.

ZAZIE. What's he saying, Sandra?

SANDRA. Electro–convulsive therapy. They give you electric shocks. In your head.

They all stare at the Doctor.

FITZPATRICK. Of course. The media has turned this whole thing into an emotional issue. All right, it's crude. But we have to face the fact that medicine is crude, even today. Take surgery. Every time the surgeon uses his knife he's inflicting a wound on his patient. He's damaging tissue. Crude stuff. But the damage he inflicts is nothing compared with the benefit to the patient in the end. And, of course, the body has wonderful recuperative powers.

SANDRA. Yes, but we're not talking about bodies. We're talking about somebody's brain.

FITZPATRICK. Yes, of course. But there's nothing to worry about in George's case. It's not as if he were down for leucotomy. Don't you worry, Mrs O'Brien. We shan't turn your husband into a vegetable.

They find this assurance less than comforting. They turn to look at Sandra for leadership. She frowns, looking down at her hands, by no means satisfied. However, she compresses her lips and says nothing.

FITZPATRICK. Well, I expect you'd like to see him.

He gets up. The others rise. Fitzpatrick moves towards Nasri, who comes forward. Doctor Bannerjee smiles at Zazie.

DOCTOR BANNERJEE. Please don't have any fears regarding electro–convulsive therapy. We have a very impressive record in this field. I am even now treating a far more acute case than that of your husband. My patient has been admitted no less than five times over the past few years and we have been very successful with him every time.

Nasri leads them off.

44. Interior. Cubicle. Day.

A very tiny room. A high window, barred. Metal attachments on the walls, presumably for the restraint of the violent. A narrow bed, a chair, a small table. A pisspot under the bed. George is curled up on the bed in foetal position, fast asleep. He wears ill-fitting, faded, hospital pyjamas. A little Party entering fills the room. They stand silent and motionless looking down at the sleeping George. Then, with a strangled cry Zazie falls to her knees beside the bed and clasps George to her. George, rudely awakened, gives a shout of terror and buries his face in his hands, squirming into the corner, out of Zazie's reach. Zazie, anguished, looks up at the others. They're staring at George in horror. George slowly turns his head. There's no sign of recognition on his face. Slowly he unwinds himself. He pushes himself into a sitting position. Zazie shrinks back as George gets slowly off the bed and, zombie-like, swaying slightly, reaches past her for his dressing-gown. He makes an awkward business of getting it on, missing the sleeve, muttering to himself. Zazie raises a hand to help, but dare not risk contact with him. George gets the dressing-gown on and sits down heavily on the edge of the bed. He looks blearily at his visitors. Lily turns to Mokwe. She speaks hoarsely:

LILY. They done it. They done it to him. They turn him into a vegetable.

> *Zazie gives a cry and falls forward, kneeling at George's feet. She clasps his hand in hers. He looks at her dazedly and gives her a weak smile. Her cry has disturbed the man in the next cubicle. He starts up a nerve-tingling, high-pitched ulululation. This seems to bring George to awareness. He shouts.*

GEORGE. Nasri ... (*Getting no answer he bellows.*) Nasri ... Nasri ...

> *Running feet are heard. All turn as Nasri appears in the doorway.*

For Christ's sake man, can't you give Maurice his shot? I got visitors, man.

> *Nasri nods and disappears. George rubs his face and shakes his head. The sounds diminish to a whimpering and then to silence.*

ZAZIE. George ... oh, George ... are you all right? Are you? I been so worried.

GEORGE. Yes, I'm all right. One or two decent fellers to talk to. The alcoholics are the best. One of the alkies is a real gentleman. A Wing Commander of the Royal Air Force. Retired, of course. A very interesting man to talk to. He's got a moustache. A big moustache out to here.

He indicates its monstrous proportions. George giggles, then looks up at them pleasantly.

Well, nice to see you. How you getting on, everyone?

They stare at him, speechless at the sight of this garrulous vegetable. George interprets their regard as condemnatory. Zazie looks down on him with compassion.

ZAZIE. We come to take you out of here. You come out of here with us. Come with me. I look after you. You be all right with me.

George shakes his head.

GEORGE. No, Zazie. I got to take this treatment. I been sick, Zazie. Sick in my head. That treatment doing me good, man. When I finish my treatment I'll come out.

He laughs.

When I come out of here I'll be a different man.

ZAZIE. I don't want you different. (*She pauses.*) You live your life the way you want, George. That's all right with me, George. You live like you want and I be with you.

GEORGE. I been having talks with the Doctor. He explained to me how I been going wrong. He tells me how I got to learn to recognise the realities of my situation.

Sandra, who has said nothing, is moved almost to tears:

SANDRA. Oh, Lord, this is terrible! It's that damnable ECT, that's what it is. (*She sits beside him and looks at him earnestly.*) George, you mustn't let them ... I mean, George, you've got such ... such energy, and although it's true we've sometimes felt ... George, you've got to refuse that treatment. You've got to withdraw your consent. They've got to stop this ECT. It's destroying your mind, George.

GEORGE. That ECT doing me good, man! I got depression, clinical depression, I got. The ECT curing me of my depression.

George considers for a moment.

Of course, it makes it hard to remember things sometimes. Oh, no, that's a bleddy good treatment. After that treatment you like a newborn baby. All you thinkin' about is when your dinner coming. That give you an appetite, that ECT.

He beams at them.

ZAZIE. How long? How long you got to stay, George?

He smiles at her.

GEORGE. I don't know, Zazie. I got a hell of a lot to forget, man. A hell of a lot to forget.

Freeze frame on George's face.

Dissolve.

45. Interior. Hospital ECT treatment room.

Close shot of George's arm. A hypodermic in it.

NASRI (*off*). Okay, George, start counting ...

GEORGE (*off*). One, two, three, four ...

As he counts George's battered face loses consciousness, a serene smile on his features. As soon as he's unconscious a female Nurse assists Nasri to place the tongue guard and electrodes in place. A Doctor bustles in and applies the current. George's body arches in a convulsion. Freeze frame on George's arched body.

Fade out.